To Kiki

Thank You For Your Support -

The Power That Lies With Your Prayers

(signature)

Jabin Sims, M.S.

The Power That Lies With Your Prayers

Jabin Sims, M.S.

All Scripture quotations are taken from the New International Version Bible.

Copyright © 2008
All Rights Reserved

PUBLISHED BY:
BRENTWOOD CHRISTIAN PRESS
4000 BEALLWOOD AVENUE
COLUMBUS, GEORGIA 31904

Contents

Have you ever been in a relationship where you and your partner did not communicate very well? More than likely, the relationship was not a fulfilling one. Many marriages end in divorce simply because of a lack of communication. If the lack of communication can cause a marriage to fall apart on earth, what do you think it will do to your relationship with your heavenly Father? If you want to have a strong, fulfilling relationship with God, you have to communicate with him on a regular basis. In this book, you will discover how effective your prayers can be.

Chapter 1

Understanding what prayer is

Prayer is simply communicating with God. I find it amazing for people to be able to communicate with the person that created the world. However, people often take this for granted for one reason or another. Prayer is something that should not be neglected because it is the link between God and us. Some people do not have a clue on how to pray or what to pray. For the next few moments, let's take a look at how you should pray. In Matthew, chapter 6, Jesus stated the following:

> *"This, then, is how you should pray 'Our Father in heaven, hallowed be your name, your kingdom come, your will be done on earth as it is in heaven. Give us today our daily bread. Forgive us our debts, as we also have forgiven our debtors. And lead us not into temptation, but deliver us from the evil one' "(Matt.6:9-13 NIV).*

The first line in this prayer indicates that you should praise God and honor His name. Whenever you praise God you are expressing how much you appreciate Him. So you should always begin your prayer with praise. The second line, "Your kingdom come" refers to God's spiritual reign. The phrase, "Your will be done" is simply stating that God's purpose will be accomplished in the world. When you pray, "Give us today our daily bread," you are acknowledging that God is the ultimate provider. There are people who think they can provide for themselves, which is not true. Only God can provide for you. "Forgive us our debts, as we forgive our debtors," actually means that we are asking God to forgive us for things we have done wrong, just as we have forgiven others. Has someone ever made you so upset that you couldn't forgive him or her? If you cannot forgive someone for hurting you, how can you expect God to forgive you when you hurt Him? You hurt God whenever you do something contrary to His Word. If you want Him to forgive you when you hurt Him, you must be forgiving when others hurt you. The final phrase, "And lead us not into temptation, but deliver us from the evil one," is stating that you should pray to be delivered from trying times and deliverance from the devil when tempted.

Christians need to learn how to pray in God's will. *"This is the confidence we have in approaching God: that if we ask anything according to his will, he hears us. And if we know that he hears us—whatever we ask—we know that we have what we asked of him" (1 John 5:14-15 NIV)*. Whenever you go to God in prayer, you do not want to approach Him by demanding what you want Him to do, instead, ask God what He wants for you. The key is to align your prayers with God's will and He will definitely answer your prayers.

What does prayer clarify for us?

Prayer illuminates the difficulties you are facing and God's ability to help you through them. Nehemiah demonstrates how to pray in the following prayer:

> *"O Lord, God of heaven, the great and awesome God, who keeps his covenant of love with those who love him and obey his commands, let your ear*

be attentive and your eyes open to hear the prayer
your servant is praying before you day and night
for your servants, the people of Israel. I confess
the sins we Israelites, including myself and my
father's house, have committed against you. We
have acted very wickedly toward you. We have not
obeyed the commands, decrees and laws you gave
your servant Moses" (Nehemiah 1:5-7 NIV).

Nehemiah's prayer demonstrates five things:
1. Praise
2. Thanksgiving
3. Repentance
4. Specific request
5. Commitment

Nehemiah's prayer was very effective because he praised God, thanked Him, repented, made a specific request, and committed to God.

Now that you have a better understanding of how to pray, the question is, when do you pray? Mark 1:35 says, *"Very early in the morning, while it was still dark, Jesus got up, left the house and went off to a solitary place, where he prayed" (NIV).* Jesus knew the importance of having a strong prayer life. He knew the obstacles He would face and He had to have a close relationship with His Father to obtain the strength to get through the trials. Notice, Jesus went off to a solitary place to pray. A solitary place is a place where you go to spend time in prayer alone. Your solitary place could be your closet, bathroom, den, etc. This place should be somewhere you can go by yourself to pray to your Heavenly Father. Why should you go by yourself to pray? Spending time alone with God not only strengthens your relationship with Him, it also prepares you to face life's struggles. That is why Jesus made no excuses to find time to pray.

This verse also says Jesus got up in the morning to pray. What is so special about praying in the morning? Communicating with God first thing in the morning allows you to be able to cast all of your worries and problems on Him and you can commit the entire day to Him. There were times in the past when I didn't pray to God in the morning and my day did not go very well. I worried myself to the point that my problems made me physically ill. However, whenever I pray first thing in the morning, I am able to free my mind of my troubles and can commit the rest of the day to Him. God is the supplier of all my needs and He is the only one who can fix my problems; that is why I make it a point to communicate with Him every morning. Now, I do not want you to misunderstand this verse. Some people may think the only time they should pray is in the morning. You can pray at anytime. However, praying in the morning is good because you can start your day with your mind on God. If there is anything bothering you, you can tell God and let Him take care of it, opposed to worrying about your problems all day.

What is spontaneous prayer?

Spontaneous prayer is simply praying at any given time. One person in the Bible who did this on a regular basis was Nehemiah.

> *"The king said to me, 'What is it you want?' Then I prayed to the God of heaven. Hear us, O our God, for we are despised. Turn their insults back on their own heads. Give them over as plunder in a land of captivity. Do not cover up their guilt or*

10

blot out their sins from your sight, for they have thrown insults in the face of the builders" (Nehemiah 4:4-5 NIV).

"Remember me with favor, O my God, for all I have done for these people" (Nehemiah 5:19 NIV).

"Remember Tobiah and Sanballat, O my God, because of what they have done; remember also the prophetess Noadiah and the rest of the prophets who have been trying to intimidate me" (Nehemiah 6:14 NIV).

Nehemiah prayed at any time. No matter what was going on around him, he would pray. Nehemiah knew the importance of a strong prayer life. No matter what is going on around you, you can pray to God at any time.

Combining prayer with preparation

"They all plotted together to come and fight against Jerusalem and stir up trouble against it. But we prayed to our God and posted a guard day and night to meet this threat" (Nehemiah 4:8-9 NIV).

Nehemiah made an effort of combining prayer with preparation. People often pray without taking the time to see what God wants them to do. When you combine prayer with preparation, you are letting God know that you are serious about what you are praying for.

Serious prayer

"So we fasted and petitioned our God about this, and he answered our prayer" (Ezra 8:23 NIV). Ezra and many

other people were about to travel approximately 900 miles on foot and they needed God to protect them. They would encounter dangerous and difficult territory on their journey and Ezra knew that. He was so serious about seeking God's protection that they proclaimed a fast and God answered their prayer. Fasting is simply going without food for a period of time so you can spend time mediating on God's word and praying.

Serious prayer requires an enormous amount of concentration. Ezra and the others were willing to neglect their need for food to get an answer from God. Fasting showed their complete dependence on God. Not only that, fasting allowed them to have more time to spend in prayer. Whenever you need to get an answer from God, you need to fast and pray just like Ezra and watch God move.

The power of prayer

"Is any one of you in trouble? He should pray. Is anyone happy? Let him sing songs of praise. Is any one of you sick? He should call the elders of the church to pray over him and anoint him with oil in the name of the Lord. And the prayer offered in faith will make the sick person well; the Lord will raise him up. If he has sinned, he will be forgiven. Therefore confess your sins to each other and pray for each other so that you may be healed. The prayer of a righteous man is powerful and effective" (James 5:13-16 NIV).

When people in the church are suffering or sick, they should know without a doubt that the elders in the church will pray for them. The elders should respond to any member who is sick at anytime.

Did you know your prayers are a part of God's healing process? James 5, verse 15 says, *"And the prayer offered in faith will make the sick person well; the Lord will raise him up"* and *verse* 16 says, *"The prayer of a righteous man is powerful and effective"(NIV).* If you are a man or woman of God, when you begin to pray in faith, God intervenes to heal the person you are praying for. There is power in prayer.

There was a young woman who had found two lumps in her breast at the age of twenty-four. She remembered what God had promised her. A couple of years ago, her mother went through the same situation and she didn't tell anybody. One night they went to a church revival and an evangelist pointed out her mother and said that her faith in God has healed her. Not only that, since her daughter praised God in the mist of that situation, she would not get cancer. Given that the daughter remembered, she brought the situation to God's attention and didn't worry about it. A couple of days later, she woke up on a Sunday morning and the two lumps in her breast were gone. She immediately started praising God for healing her.

Why people are afraid to talk with God

As crazy as it may sound, people are often afraid to talk with God. Isaiah 7:12 says, *"But Ahaz said, 'I will not ask; I will not put the Lord to the test' "* (NIV). The reason why Ahaz made that statement was because he did not want to know what God would say. God told him to ask for a sign. *"Again the Lord spoke to Ahaz, 'Ask the Lord your God for a sign, whether in the deepest depths or in the highest heights' "* (Isaiah 7:10-11 NIV). People often make excuses for not talking with God because they do not want to know what God will say. One of my friends avoided asking God what his calling was because of the dreams he was having. In his dreams, he would be preaching to large groups of people in the church. He was terrified to speak in front of people because he always thought they would make fun of him. Although he wasn't sure if God wanted him to preach, he did not want to pray to God because he did not want to be a preacher.

If you feel that God is telling you to do something, don't be afraid to ask Him. As a matter of fact, God wants you to ask. You may try to prevent knowing the truth about what God wants you to do. However, God is all knowing, He knows your motives. He knows if you are trying to avoid what He wants you to do. If you do that, you will suffer the consequences for running from Him. When God told Jonah to go and preach to the city of Nineveh, Jonah tried to run by sailing to Tarshish. Little did he know, that God is everywhere at the same time. So there was no way Jonah could run from God and escape. Because he disobeyed Him, God caused a severe storm to take place:

> *"Then the Lord sent a great wind on the sea, and such a violent storm arose that the ship threatened to break up" (Jonah 1:4 NIV).*

God sent Jonah a wake up call and at the end of the day Jonah did what God had told him to do. To avoid being punished for being disobedient, just do what God tells you to.

What to request from God in prayer

When people pray, they often do not know what to request from God. So, let's look at Solomon's prayer in 1 Kings 8:56-61:

> *"Praise be to the Lord, who has given rest to his people Israel just as he promised. Not one word has failed of all the good promises he gave*

through his servant Moses. May the Lord our God be with us as he was with our fathers; may he never leave us nor forsake us. May he turn our heart to him, to walk in all his ways and to keep the commands, decrees and regulations he gave our fathers. And may these words of mine, which I have prayed before the Lord, be near to the Lord our God day and night, that he may uphold the cause of his servant and the cause of his people Israel according to each day's need, so that all the peoples of the earth may know that the Lord is God and that there is no other. But your hearts must be fully committed to the Lord our God, to live by his decrees and obey his commands, as at this time" (NIV).

Solomon's prayer consisted of five basic requests: (1) the presence of God (verse 57); (2) to do God's will (verse 58); (3) for His help on each day's need (verse 59); (4) the ability to obey God's commands, decrees, and regulations (verse 58); (5) for God's kingdom to spread all over the world (verse 60). Whenever you pray for your friends, family, or church, you can present these requests to God just as Solomon did.

Daniels' disciplined prayer life

Daniel 6:10-12 says, *"Now when Daniel learned that the decree had been published, he went home to his upstairs room where the windows opened toward Jerusalem. Three times a day he got down on his knees and prayed, giving thanks to his God, just as he had done before. Then these men went as a group and found Daniel praying and asking God for help. So they went to the king and spoke to him about his royal decree: 'Did you not publish a decree that during the next thirty days anyone who prays to any god or man except to you, O king, would be thrown into the lions' den?' The king answered, ' The decree stands—in accordance with the laws of the Medes and Persians, which cannot be repealed' " (NIV).*

There was a law that stated that no one was supposed to pray to any god or man except to the king or they would be thrown into the lion's den. No matter what the law said, Daniel prayed to God three times a day. Daniel knew God was the only one who could give him the strength and guidance he needed in his life.

Our prayers are usually interrupted by the affairs of life—work schedules, school schedules, etc. But, praying to God is something that needs to be done on a regular basis because it is the lifeline of our relationship with Him.

Prayer is more effective than your crisis

It is very easy for people to panic about a situation in their lives. As soon as their finances run out, they wonder how they are going to pay the bills. As soon as they find out that they have a severe disease, they panic. As soon as they find out that they are going to lose their home, they panic. The world we live in is not an easy place to live. There is so much that can cause people to lose hope. Whenever you are faced with an unpleasant situation, take it to God in prayer. In Daniel, chapter 2, Daniel was hit with a crisis:

"At this, Daniel went in to the king and asked for time, so that he might interpret the dream for him. Then Daniel returned to his house and explained the mater to his friends Hananiah, Mishael and Azariah. He urged them to plead for

mercy from the God of heaven concerning this mystery, so that he and his friends might not be executed with the rest of the wise men of Babylon" (Daniel 2:16-18 NIV).

Daniel and his friends were going to be killed if Daniel could not interpret a dream for King Nebuchadnezzar. If someone told you that you would be killed if you could not interpret a particular dream, how would you respond? Most folks would panic if something like that were to take place. But Daniel did not panic. He went to his three friends and had a prayer meeting. After they prayed, God revealed His answer to Daniel that night. *"During the night the mystery was revealed to Daniel in a vision" (Daniel 2:19 NIV).* Whenever you encounter any kind of situation, don't panic; instead, take the situation to God in prayer.

How you can pray for others

Have you ever had a desire to pray for your friends, family, church leaders, but didn't know how? In Colossians 1:9-14, Paul lays out the formula for praying for others:

"For this reason, since the day we heard about you, we have not stopped praying for you and asking God to fill you with the knowledge of his will through all spiritual wisdom and under-standing. And we pray this in order that you may live a life worthy of the Lord and may please him in every way: bearing fruit in every good work, growing in the knowledge of God, being strength-ened with all power according to his glorious might so that you may have great endurance and patience, and joyfully giving thanks to the Father,

who has qualified you to share in the inheritance of the saints in the kingdom of light. For he has rescued us from the dominion of darkness and brought us into the kingdom of the Son he loves, in whom we have redemption, the forgiveness of sins" (NIV).

Whenever you want to pray for someone you can request that they understand God's will, gain spiritual wisdom, please and honor God, bear good fruit, grow in the knowledge of God, be filled with God's strength, have great endurance and patience, stay full of Christ's joy, and always give thanks. Paul's prayer pattern is an excellent source on how to pray for others.

In addition, you need to be able to pray for government leaders. *"I urge, then, first of all, that requests, prayers, intercession and thanksgiving be made for everyone—for kings and all those in authority, that we may live peaceful and quiet lives in all godliness and holiness. This is good, and pleases God our Savior, who wants all men to be saved and to come to a knowledge of the truth" (1 Timothy 2:1-4 NIV).* One thing that you do not want to do is to take the government for granted. Make a habit of praying for government leaders daily. This is something that pleases the Lord because He wants all men to be saved and to know the truth.

Also, there is a need for you to pray for Christian leaders. Hebrews 13:18-19 says, *"Pray for us. We are sure that we have a clear conscience and desire to live honorably in every way. I particularly urge you to pray so that I may be restored to you soon" (NIV).* Christian leaders are not exempt from satanic attacks. In 2 Samuel 11, David saw a woman taking a bath and he sent someone to inquire of her.

The person he sent told David that the woman he was looking at was married. However, David did not care if the woman was married or not. He did not resist the temptation of sleeping with her, nor did he pray to God for strength to resist temptation. If he had taken the time to ask for strength, he would not have fallen into sexual immorality because God would have provided a way for him to escape temptation.

Christians need to pray when people hurt them. When someone has wronged you for one reason or another, do not get revenge by doing something ungodly to him or her. Instead, pray for those who have wronged you. *"Do not repay evil with evil or insult with insult, but with blessing, because to this you were called so that you may inherit a blessing" (1 Peter 3:9 NIV).*

Christians need to pray for their children. *"When a period of feasting had run its course, Job would send and have them purified. Early in the morning he would sacrifice a burnt offering for each of them, thinking, 'Perhaps my children have sinned and cursed God in their hearts' " (Job 1:5 NIV).* Job offered sacrifices for his children because he was afraid that they might have sinned unknowingly. He was very concerned about his children's spiritual welfare. Parents need to pray for their children. This shows that they are concerned about their spiritual welfare. Parents can also sacrifice their time by asking God to protect them, to honor and please Him, to grow spiritually and much more.

People often wonder if failing to pray for others is a sin. Let's look at 1 Samuel 12:23, *"As for me, far be it from me that I should sin against the Lord by failing to pray for you. And I will teach you the way that is good and right" (NIV).* According to Samuel, Christians are required to pray for others and they are to teach others to do good.

Intercessory prayer

"Pray for the peace of Jerusalem: 'May those who love you be secure. May there be peace within your walls and security within your citadels.' For the sake of my brothers and friends, I will say, 'Peace be within you.' For the sake of the house of the Lord our God, I will seek your prosperity" (Psalm 122:6-9 NIV).

The psalmist who wrote this psalm was David. He prayed on behalf of the people in Jerusalem. This is called the Intercessory Prayer because he prayed for the needs of others rather than his own needs and desires. Do you have a friend or family member that is suffering mentally, physically, or spiritually? Intercede on their behalf today.

The prayers of the believers' in the Bible are a model for us.

"On their release, Peter and John went back to their own people and reported all that the chief priests and elders had said to them. When they heard this, they raised their voices together in prayer to God. 'Sovereign Lord,' they said, 'you made the heaven and the earth and the sea, and everything in them. You spoke by the Holy Spirit through the mouth of your servant, our father David: Why do the nations rage and the peoples plot in vain? The Kings of the earth take their stand and the rulers gather together against the Lord and against his Anointed One.' Indeed Herod and Pontius Pilate met together with the Gentiles and the people of Israel in this city to conspire against your holy servant Jesus, whom

you anointed. They did what your power and will had decided beforehand should happen. Now, Lord, consider their threats and enable your servants to speak your word with great boldness. Stretch out your hand to heal and perform miraculous signs and wonders through the name of your holy servant Jesus. After they prayed, the place where they were meeting was shaken. And they were all filled with the Holy Spirit and spoke the word of God boldly" (Acts 4:23-31 NIV).

The first thing the believers' did was to praise God. They began their prayer with praise. Notice this, " *'Sovereign Lord,' they said, you made the heaven and the earth and the sea, and everything in them. You spoke by the Holy Spirit through the mouth of your servant, our father David" (Acts 4:24-25 NIV).* They praised God for His creation before anything else. After they praised God, then they told God their problem.

"Why do the nations rage and the peoples plot in vain? The Kings of the earth take their stand and the rulers gather together against the Lord and against his Anointed One" (Acts 4:25-26 NIV.)

Notice that in this entire text, these believers' did not ask God to remove their problem; instead, they asked God to help them deal with it.

The third thing that these believers' did was that they asked God for boldness.

"Now, Lord, consider their threats and enable your servants to speak your word with great boldness" (Acts 4:29 NIV).

In order to be bold you have to have courage. You will not let fear keep you from standing up for what is right. If you are not a bold person for the Lord, ask God for boldness just like these believers did.

The fourth thing these believers did after they prayed was to allow God to answer them.

> *"After they prayed, the place where they were meeting was shaken. And they were all filled with the Holy Spirit and spoke the word of God boldly" (Acts 4:31 NIV).*

After you have prayed about your situation, wait for God to answer you. God may answer you immediately like He did with these believers, or He may delay His answer, but in either case, thank God for hearing your prayers.

When to stop praying and get moving

"Then the Lord said to Moses, 'Why are you crying out to me? Tell the Israelites to move on' " (Exodus 14:15 NIV). There comes a time when you need to stop praying and take action. Moses continued to pray to God without taking any action and God told him to get moving. People often use prayer as an excuse not to take action for the very thing they were praying for.

One of my old classmates complained that he could not find a job and he was about to lose his car. He told me that he had been praying for a month and could not find anything. I asked him how many jobs did he apply for and he told me none. He was praying for a job, but he did not take any action by filling out any applications. There is a time when you need to pray and there is a time when you need to take action.

Prayers help us remember God's goodness

"When you have eaten and are satisfied, praise the Lord your God for the good land he has given you" *(Deuteronomy 8:10 NIV).* People often wonder why we say grace before and after meals. The purpose of saying grace is to praise the Lord for the meals that He has blessed you with. This verse is a reminder not to forget God when He has fulfilled your needs.

Chapter 2

Prayer can help you overcome temptation

As long as you live on this earth, you will be tempted in one way or another to sin. People often fall into temptation because they do not use the key ingredient to overcome it, which is prayer. Matthew 26:41 says, *"Watch and pray so that you will not fall into temptation. The spirit is willing, but the body is weak" (NIV)*. Temptation often strikes areas where you are vulnerable. If you are feeling lonely, depressed, discouraged, have marital, relationship problems, hopelessness etc., you will be tempted to do things that are wrong. I remember when a young lady came to me for comfort because her boyfriend had cheated on her. She did everything she could to please him and he still ended up cheating. This young lady was in a vulnerable state of mind because she had been hurt. As a result, she started coming on to me because I was a great listener. I told her that I could not go there with her because I was a born again Christian and I would not feel right taking advantage of her. Whenever you are in a vulnerable state, Satan will tempt you to sin.

In the first chapter of the book of Samuel, Hannah, the wife of Elkanah, was discourage because she was unable to have children and everybody made fun of her. This affected Hannah to the point of being physically ill and unable to eat. Hannah cried out to the Lord for a child saying, *"O Lord Almighty, if you will only look upon your servant's misery and remember me, and not forget your servant but give her*

24

a son, then I will give him to the Lord for all the days of his life, and no razor will ever be used on his head" (1 Samuel 1:11 NIV). After Hannah poured out her heart to God, the Lord blessed her with a son.

Prayer is a powerful tool that will help you overcome temptation.

I was once asked, "Does God tempt people?" The answer is no. God does not tempt anyone and He cannot be tempted by evil. Satan is the one who tempts you. He does not want anyone to live the way God intends, so he will do everything that he can to achieve that. In the beginning, Satan tempted Eve and succeeded in getting her to sin. Ever since then, he has been on a rampage. Did you know that Eve could have resisted temptation? In Genesis 3:1-6, Satan tempted Eve to eat fruit from the tree that was in the middle of the garden. The first thing he did was to get her to doubt Gods goodness. He stated that God was stingy for not wanting Eve to share his knowledge of good and evil. He caused Eve to focus her attention on something that she couldn't have. Whenever you doubt God's goodness and focus your attention on the things that you don't have, Satan will use that to get you to sin. Not once did Eve pray when tempted to sin. If she had prayed, she would have been able to overcome that temptation.

There have been occasions where Satan tempted me to say things to people that was not godly. However, prayer has helped me to control my speech. Several years ago, I worked for a trucking company that did not treat me right. The company's administrators often gave me the worst loads that were available and saved the best loads for people that they liked. After putting up with them for four months, I decided to put in my two-week notice. They told me that they were not going to accept a two notice. I told them that I wanted to work for two more weeks because I had some financial obligations that I had to take care of. They told me that they did not care what I had to take care of and for me to return the truck.

That really upset me because I needed to take care of my obligations. Not only that, I was in the state of Alabama when they told me to return the truck and I was living in Michigan at the time. So I am thinking to myself, "how in the world am I going to get home." I did not have any money and I could not borrow money from anyone. Instead of saying hurtful words to those people, I had to ask God to help me not to say anything that would be disrespectful to them. As I prayed to God, I asked Him to give me strength to endure the situation and He did just that. But, I still had a problem. I did not have a way to get back home. At the time, I had two credit cards and I was sure that they were maxed out. But something kept telling me to call the credit card companies and find out the balances. The first company I called told me that the card had reached its limit. The second company that I called told me that I had an available credit line of $300. My mouth had dropped to the floor. That was more than enough for me to get a rental car to get home. All I can say is that the Lord will provide. Not only did prayer give me strength to endure bad treatment, God also provided a way for me to get home safely.

There was a young lady who fell deeply in love with a man who was striving to fulfill his God-given purpose. Before she had met this man, her life was heading in the wrong direction. She drank, obtained body piercing, used profanity, engaged in pre-marital sex, and she gambled. One day in Chicago, Illinois, she went over to a friend's because they had previously made plans to hang out. She had no idea that making that visit would change her life forever.

When she arrived at her friends' house, she was introduced to her friends' cousin who was a minister. Some how, the minister was able to see into this woman's heart. He knew that she had been raised up in church since birth, but she had gone astray. He felt that she wanted to get her life back on track, but she did not know where to start. After talking with this woman for about two hours, he asked her if she wanted to give her life back to God. She said that she really wanted to, but did not know where to begin. He told her that all she had to do was pray the sinner's prayer and her relationship with God would be restored. After they prayed, the minister invited her to church that following Sunday.

That Saturday, while she was alone at work, one of her ex-boyfriend's decided to come to her job to engage in sexual activity. She knew that she needed God's help to overcome that temptation, so she started praying in her heart. Given that she prayed, God gave her the strength to tell her ex-boyfriend that it was over and he needed to leave the premises. When she arrived at church the next day, she told the minister how God gave her the power to get through her situation. Since then, they have been dating.

Chapter 3

Turn Your Worries Into Prayers

Have you ever had problems with your finances, family, friends, job, health, etc? These are just some of the things that cause people to worry. Worrying can have detrimental affects on your health. I remember a young lady I once dated had the worst attitude that I've ever seen. She complained about everything under the sun. Once we broke up, she started stalking me. Not only that, she told people things about me that were not true. I began to worry about what people thought about me. I started worrying about my reputation. I didn't want people to think the things this woman was saying about me was true, when it wasn't. I worried myself to the point that I got sick and almost had to go to the hospital. There were many times when I was driving that I ran off the road because I couldn't think clearly. I tried to be strong through the situation but I couldn't deal with the fact that my reputation was being destroyed. It took so long to build a name for myself and for someone to plant lies about me literally made me sick.

Another incident that happened with me was when God had blessed me to purchase a semi-truck. I saved for quite some time just for the down payment. Everything went very well for about seven months. In the eighth month, everything started going wrong with the truck. When I took it to the shop, the mechanic told me that it will cost $10,000 to repair the truck. I said to myself, "where am I going to get $10,000?" I did not have the money to get the truck fixed. So I called the company that I was leased to and I asked if I could borrow some money to get my truck fixed and they could just take the money out of my check every week until they were paid. They said no. Then I contacted the bank that I was financing my truck through and they told me I had not had the truck long enough to refinance it. Everything that I tried to do to get my truck fixed didn't work and eventually I lost the truck.

One thing that I failed to do in both cases was to pray. Prayer should have been my first priority. Instead of praying about the situation and putting it in God's hands, I decided to fix the situation myself and both times I failed. People often try to take matters into their own hands and wonder why they fail. God is omniscient, which means he knows all. He knows your financial struggles, your trials, and your pains. He wants you to bring all those issues to Him in prayer. Paul said in Philippians 4:6, "Do not be anxious about anything, but in everything by prayer and petition with thanksgiving present your requests to God" (NIV). Whenever you are faced with a situation go to God in prayer. In Genesis 32:9, Jacob prayed to God because he was about to face his brother Esau for the first time in twenty-years. When they were younger Jacob stole Esau's birthright, a special honor that the first-born son received. Although Jacob was afraid, he took his problem to God in prayer. God can fix anything in your life if you will just let Him.

In South Bend, Indiana, a lady walked to her car to leave for work, but there was a man who wanted to rob her. He punched her in the face, snatched her purse, and ran off. She screamed as loud as she could but no one came to her rescue. After the crime, she was terrified to walk out to her vehicle if it was dark outside. She was so worried that someone would try to rob her. She would catch rides to work, have family members walk her out to her vehicle every morning, and have people to watch her go home at night. Soon, her fear disrupted her family because they were always accommodating her. One day, her daughter told her that the only person that could give her the ability to stop worrying about being attacked again was God. After a year of consistent prayer, this lady was able to walk out to her car with no problem, no matter how dark it was outside.

Here are seven reasons not to worry (NIV):

Matthew 6:25	The same God who created life in you can be trusted with the details of your life.
Matthew 6:26	Worrying about the future affects your efforts for today.
Matthew 6:27	Worrying is more harmful than helpful.
Matthew 6:28-30	God does not ignore those who depend on him.
Matthew 6:31,32	Worry shows a lack of faith in and understanding of God.
Matthew 6:33	There are real challenges God wants us to pursue, and worrying keeps us from them.
Matthew 6:34	Living one day at a time keeps us from being consumed with worry.

Christians know that they should not worry, but they do. Many of them worry themselves to the point that they will start complaining to God about their situation. Not once do they think to pray instead of complaining. And if they do pray about their situation, many of them get upset if God does not respond when they want Him to. In Exodus 17:2, the Israelites complained to Moses because they were thirsty. There was no water in Rephidim. They could not understand why Moses took them to a place to die of thirst. Instead of the Israelites taking their problem to God in prayer, they complained. Whenever you have a problem, don't complain. Pray to God and ask Him for help.

Chapter 4

Common Problems In Prayer

Have you ever prayed to God and wondered why you did not receive what you prayed for? In the book of James, he states why God does not answer prayer. He says, *"You want something but don't get it. You kill and covet, but you cannot have what you want. You quarrel and fight. You do not have, because you do not ask God. When you ask, you do not receive, because you ask with wrong motives, that you may spend what you get on your pleasures" (James 4:2-3 NIV).* The most common problems in prayer are asking for the wrong things, not asking at all, or asking for the wrong reasons.

Whenever you pray, do you pray only to satisfy your personal desires? If so, that may be the reason why God is not answering your prayers. Many people want more money, more cars, more homes, more recognition, etc. People are willing to fight to get what they want no matter what. These are selfish desires that come from within. God wants you to submit yourself totally to him. He will provide you with what you need. Matthew 6:33 says, *"But seek first his kingdom and his righteousness, and all these things will be given to you as well" (NIV).* What are these things: Food, clothing, shelter, etc. Whatever you need, God will provide. However, you must submit yourself to Him and trust that He will do what He said He will.

Also, some people feel like they shouldn't have to ask God for anything since He already knows everything. I met a man who was struggling to find a job. He had two kids, a boy and a girl. Their mother was killed in a car accident, so he didn't have anyone to help him care for his children. The man was so frustrated that he started contemplating suicide. I asked the man, "Have you asked God to help you find a job." He said, "No. God knows that I need a job; so I shouldn't have to ask." I said, "God may know that you need a job; however, He is waiting on you to ask him." After talking with Him for an hour, we prayed that God would bless him with a job. That following week, he found a job.

Whenever you pray to God, you must pray with the right motives. You cannot ask God to bless you with a higher paying job, when your intentions are to spend the money on alcohol and drugs. If you want a better vehicle to drive, but your intentions are to show off your car to people who cannot afford one, God will not honor your prayer request. Therefore, whatever you ask for, it must be with the right motives.

Chapter 5

Does God hear my prayers?

Do you ever wonder if God can hear your prayers, especially when you are going through hard times? I want you to know that God does hear your prayers. Psalm 4:3 says, *"Know that the Lord has set apart the godly for himself; the Lord will hear when I call to him" (NIV).* The godly are those people who are faithful to God. If you have trusted Christ as your Lord and Savior, God will listen to your prayers. In this scripture, David knew with no doubt in his mind that God would hear his prayers.

In addition, you need to continue to pray when you feel like God is far away. I remember when an individual said to me, "I do not know if God can hear my prayers because he seems so far away." Have you ever felt as if God was so far away that it was impossible for Him to hear your prayers? Everything is not what it seems to be. You may feel God is far away, but He's not. Whenever you get this feeling, make sure you pray consistently. In Psalm 10:1, David said, *"Why, O Lord, do you stand far off? Why do you hide yourself in times of trouble?" (NIV).* David had felt like God was far away because he wanted God to hurry to his aid. However, David never stopped praying, and you must do the same.

At some point of time, I'm sure you needed God to respond immediately to your situation. However, God will respond in His own time. Galatians 4:4-5 says, *"But when the time had fully come, God sent his Son, born of a woman, born under law, to redeem those under law, that we might receive the full rights of sons" (NIV).* God sent His precious Son Jesus to die for the sins of the world. The time that He sent His Son to die was perfect. Just as God knew when to send His Son to die on the cross, He knows when to answer your prayers. It's hard for many people to understand because they expect to get immediate answers. Sometimes, God will make people wait because they are not ready for what they asked Him for.

We live in a world where we expect things to happen instantly. People tend to get impatient when they are told to wait more than three or more minutes to get their food at a fast food restaurant. Have you ever noticed at the grocery store that people tend to look for the shortest check-out line? The reason being is simply because they want to get out of the store as quickly as possible. Sometimes waiting is best because the results will be positive. For instance, you went to the store and purchased a steak and instead of waiting for the steak to be cooked thoroughly, you decided to take the steak out of the package and eat it while it was raw. Nine times out of ten, you will get sick from eating a raw steak. However, if you had waited for the steak to be thoroughly cooked, the chances of you getting ill or getting a disease will be lessened. Whenever you do something prematurely, ninety-nine percent of the time you will reap a negative result. One thing about God is that His timing is perfect. When there is perfect timing, the results are positive.

In 2 Chronicles, chapter 6, Solomon prayed, but God did not answer his prayer of dedication until a long period of time had passed. In, 2 Chronicles, chapter 7, while Solomon was waiting on an answer, several other buildings were built. Finally, God told Solomon He heard his prayer.

Although God may not answer you right away, it doesn't mean He didn't hear your prayer. You must trust that God will answer you at the proper time.

When God decides to answer your prayer, don't be surprised.

In the twelfth chapter of Acts, King Herod arrested Peter for being a Christian. He was thrown into prison and was guarded by several soldiers. While Peter was in prison the church was praying for him. The night before Peter was going to be brought to trial; an angel appeared to him and woke him up. Immediately the chains that were on Peter's wrist fell off. The angel lead him safely passed the guards and out of the prison. Peter went straight to Mary's house and knocked on the door. A servant girl named Rhoda came to the door and immediately recognized Peter's voice. She ran back to tell the others who was at the door. The people told Rhoda that she had lost her mind. They believed that Peter's angel was the one at the door. So when they decided to open the door, they were amazed that Peter had managed to escape from prison.

Whenever believers come together to pray, do not be surprise when God moves. The people were praying for Peter, but they reacted like God was not going to answer their prayers. They should not have been shocked when Peter showed up. They should have had faith that God would answer their prayers. Whenever you pray something, believe that God will answer.

Reasons why God may not answer your prayers

One sure way to know that God will not answer your prayers is by disobeying Him. 1 Samuel 28:15 says,

"Samuel said to Saul, 'why have you disturbed me by bringing me up?' 'I am in great distress,' said Saul. 'The Philistines are fighting against me, and God has turned away from me. He no longer answers me, either by prophets or by dreams. So I have called on you to tell what to do' "(NIV).

God did not answer Saul's prayers because he was very disobedient. Obedience is a very crucial obligation that you have to uphold; if not, God will not hear you when you call on Him.

God will not answer your prayers if you have a problem or grievance with others. *"I want men everywhere to lift up holy hands, without anger or disputing" (1 Timothy 2:8 NIV).* If you are angry with someone, God will not hear your prayers until you settle the problem with that person. That is the main reason why Jesus said in Matthew 5:23-24, *"if you are offering your gift at the altar and there remember that your brother has something against you, leave your gift there in front of the altar. First go and be reconciled to your brother; then come and offer your gift" (NIV).* God does not like broken relationships because that can hinder your relationship with Him. The attitude that you have toward other people reflects your relationship with God. That is why it so important to resolve your problems with others so your relationship with God will not be broken.

How to respond to answered prayer

There are three ways that God will respond to your prayers. He will either say yes, no, or wait. In either case, you must accept His answer with humility.

There are times when God will say yes to your prayers. After praying to God concerning Nebuchadnezzar's dream in Daniel 2:19-23, Daniel praised God for answering his prayer. Before he rushed to tell others about what God did, he took time out to thank God for answering his prayer.

There was a man in a church that I used to belong to who had a burning desire for a wife. He prayed that the woman would be a wife of noble character, like the woman of Proverbs 31. After praying to God, he remembered that he had to wash his clothes for the following week. He walked down to the laundry room where he happened to meet a young lady. After engaging in conversation with her, he felt like this woman would be someone that he could get to know personally. Giving that he was shy, he did not ask her for her phone number. After he finished washing his clothes he went back into his apartment and prayed to God. He asked God that if that was the woman for him, have her to come down to his apartment. The very next day the power went out. Fifteen minutes later there was a knock at his door. The person that stood at the door was the young lady who he had met in the laundry room. She was wondering if her apartment was the only unit that was without power. But he knew God had caused everything to take place.

There are times when God will say no to your prayers. In 1 Chronicles 22:7-10, God told David that he could not build the temple and David told his son, Solomon: *"'My son, I had it in my heart to build a house for the Name of the Lord my God. But this word of the Lord came to me: 'You have shed much blood and have fought many wars. You are not to build a house for my Name, because you have shed much blood on the earth in my sight. But you will have a son who will be a man of peace and rest, and I will give him rest from all his enemies on every side. His name will be Solomon, and I will grant Israel peace and quiet during his reign. He is the one who will build a house for my name. He will be my son, and I will be his father. And I will establish the throne of his kingdom over Israel forever' " (NIV).* In this scripture, David accepted the fact that his son Solomon would be the one to build the temple. Most people would get upset or jealous if God had asked someone else to do a particular job. Although David wanted to build the temple himself, he did not get angry or jealous that God designated Solomon for the job. Instead, he made preparations for Solomon to fulfill his assignment.

A young man who lived in Knoxville, Tennessee wanted a promotion on his job. He was working in the area of sales and had a desire to become a sales manager. There was another person who was striving to be a sales manager as well. Giving that he had competition, he did everything he could possible do to get the position. He met all the weekly sales, went out of his way to help customers, and put in additional hours to show that he was willing to do anything to get the promotion. He constantly prayed to God for the promotion. The gentleman was extremely disappointed when the general manager made his decision. He chose the other candidate. The funny thing about this situation is that the person that he was up against was not a good worker. The reason why he didn't get the job was not so much that he was not qualified, but because he was not paying his tithes. As a result of him not paying his tithes, God said no to his prayer. His response to God's answer was not good. He cursed God and told Him how wrong He was for not allowing him to get the promotion. Given that he responded in a negative way, the man lost his job a month later.

The assurance of answered prayer brings peace
"I lie down and sleep; I wake again, because the Lord sustains me" (Psalm 3:5 NIV).

In the 3rd division of Psalm, David cried out to the Lord because of his son Absalom. Absalom had rebelled and gathered an army to kill him. Although his son was seeking to kill him, David slept peacefully.

Have you ever been in a crisis and could not sleep? One of my friends' mother had a son who was in and out of prison for fifteen years. Ten out of those fifteen years, his mother was not able to sleep at night. She used to always worry that he would get treated badly. Not only that, her son had a bad temper and he did not know how to control it. The guards would mess with him just to get him to do something stupid so that he would get more time. After ten years of worrying and developing a serious case of diabetes, she finally gave that situation over to the Lord. After praying to God about her son, she was able to sleep at night because God gave her full assurance that He was in control of circumstances.

Chapter 6

Prayer can change your situation

"In those days Hezekiah became ill and was at the point of death. The prophet Isaiah son of Amoz went to him and said, 'This is what the Lord says: Put your house in order, because you are going to die; you will not recover.' Hezekiah turned his face to the wall and prayed to the Lord, 'Remember, O Lord, how I have walked before you faithfully and with wholehearted devotion and have done what is good in your eyes.' And Hezekiah wept bitterly. Then the word of the Lord came to Isaiah: 'Go and tell Hezekiah, This is what the Lord, the God of your father David, says: I have heard your prayers and seen your tears; I will add fifteen years to your life' " (Isaiah 38:1-5 NIV).

If a man of God told you that in the next two weeks, you are going to die and you will not recover, what would be your response? Hezekiah turned to the Lord because he knew that God was the only one who could prolong his life. There are many people in this world who will literally give up on life whenever they receive bad news. They feel like there is no more hope. Many people feel that if God really loves them, He would not have allowed sickness to take over their body. If God really loves them, He would not have allowed their children to be so rebellious. If God

41

really loves them, He would not have allowed their marriage to fall apart. As a result, people often blame God for their problems. Their attitude is that God knows everything that is going on and He has the power to prevent all of their problems; yet, He is not doing anything to prevent them. This is not the way God's people should respond to problems.

If you are in a bad situation and you want God to change it you must meet a certain criteria. However, what I am about to share with you is not a guarantee that God will change your present situation because He may be using it to teach you or to grow you etc., but these conditions must be met if God does decide to change your situation.

The first thing that Hezekiah did when he was told that he was going to die was to pray. Prayer was not the last thing on Hezekiah's mind but it was the first. Whenever you encounter any problems, the first thing that you need to do is to take that problem to God in prayer. The second thing that Hezekiah did was that he reminded God how faithful he had been. The question that you need to ask yourself is, "have I been faithful to God?" The third thing that Hezekiah did was that he walked before the Lord wholeheartedly. Are you serving the Lord halfheartedly or wholeheartedly? God does not want half of your heart. He does want you to give half of your heart to the world and half to Him. So if you are serving Him halfheartedly, repent and give Him your whole heart. The fourth thing that Hezekiah did was that he did good in the sight of the Lord's eyes. Are you doing good before the Lord? God wants you to do good before Him and not evil.

Therefore, if you want God to change your present situation you need to do what Hezekiah did:

1. Pray to God
2. Be faithful to God
3. Serve God wholeheartedly
4. Do good in His sight

There was a young lady who's name was Christina who had an older brother who was in and out of prison for ten years. Christina had asked her brother over and over to go to church with her and finally he did. On the day that he finally decided to go to church, Christina had to give a testimony on how she got saved. As she was talking about how the Lord saved her and why people should be saved, her brother got offended. Her brother got upset and started walking out the church. Before he had reached the exit door, she said, "Tim, do not go outside those doors. If you do, you will be killed. Please! Stay in here." Tim did not listen. As he opened the doors and made his way down the steps a red mustang pulled up in front of the church where Tim was standing and shot him. Christina immediately woke up and poured her heart out to the Lord for Tim to be saved. That morning she got up and went to her brother's room and asked him for the twentieth time if he would go to church with her. He finally agreed that he would go.

When they got to church, Christina got up and started talking about being saved. Her brother became upset because of his convictions over the lifestyle he was living. As he was making his way towards the exit, Christina said, "Tim, do not go outside those doors or you will be killed. Please! Stay in here." Tim did not listen. When everybody saw that Tim was going to walk out the door, they began to pray. When Tim's hand touched the doorknob he was immediately paralyzed. He fell straight to the floor and could not move any part of his body. Christina ran to Tim and said to him, "you must give your life to God. Do you believe that Jesus Christ died for you." Tim said, "yes." Christina said, "Do you accept him as your Lord and savior." Tim said, "yes." Everyone in the church began to praise God. That day was the happiest day of Christina's life. She was so thankful that God had saved her brother.

There was a deacon in the church named Calvin who had been married to his wife for ten years. His wife treated him like a king. As time went on, Calvin started losing interest in her. Now his wife, Melody did not do anything to cause Calvin to feel that way. As a result of him losing interest in his wife, he started looking at other women. He didn't want to commit adultery, but he had a burning desire to be with another woman. He was literally battling his flesh. It seemed like everyday he would get more of a desire to be with other women. Nobody in the church or outside the church knew what was going on with him. Calvin was struggling so bad that whenever his wife was not at home, he would put in porn videos. Not only that, they had some neighbors down the street that he would always watch. However, he would not approach them or say anything to them, but he would always keep his eye on them. He struggled with this for quite some time.

One day when Melody went out of town for a business meeting. The neighbor that the deacon had his eye-on knocked on his door. When he opened up the door and saw that it was his neighbor, he noticed that something was wrong because of the expression that she had on her face. So he invited her into his home and they sat down on the couch. Calvin had asked his neighbor, Jessica, what was wrong. She told him that the man that she loved cheated on her. This was something that broke her heart and she needed someone to talk to. She could not think of anywhere else to go but to Calvin's house. Calvin was there to comfort the young lady. He tried to help her the best way he could. This lady had no idea that Calvin had his eye on her. He said some very encouraging words to her that really made her want to engage into sexual activity with him. Given that she was so vulnerable, she was willing to do anything to get over her pain. She started coming on to him. On one hand, Calvin was happy because she was a beautiful woman; but on the other hand, he didn't want anything to happen because he was a married man and it would be wrong to take advantage of this woman. As she was coming on to him, his wife came home. The meeting that his wife was supposed to be at was canceled, so she came back home early. As she walked in the room where Calvin and Jessica were, she began to get the feeling that something was going on. She couldn't prove it but she just had this feeling. Jessica started talking with his wife about her situation and later on that night Jessica went home. As Calvin and his wife Melody was getting ready to go to bed, she asked him if he desired to be with other women. Calvin told her that he didn't. He told her that she was the only one he ever wanted to be with. The reason why Calvin told his wife that he didn't desire to be with other women was because he did not want to hurt her feelings. He knew that his wife was a very emotional woman, therefore, he did not want to hurt her feelings.

His wife heard what he said, but she did not take it to heart because of what she saw. She didn't actually see them kissing but it was just a real awkward feeling that she had when she had walked in on them. After that, she started feeling insecure about herself. She went to work the next day and one of the men that she had worked with noticed that something was wrong with her. He knew because her work habits had started changing. She wasn't working as hard as she normally did. She was making many mistakes on her job and he knew that something was wrong. So he told her that whatever she was going through just put it in God's hands and He would work it out.

As Melody was on her way home, she happened to see her husband's car parked over at Jessica's house. Many things started running through her head. She couldn't understand why Calvin was at this woman's house. She didn't turn around and go back to Jessica's house because she wanted to see what her husband would say, so she waited until he got home. She made it in the house about 6:00 pm and started preparing dinner as she waited for Calvin. However, he did not arrive until 9:30 pm. She asked him where he had been and he said that he went to Jessica's house because he needed to fix her plumbing. Then Melody asked him why she didn't call a plumber? Calvin told her that she was having financial problems and she was not able to afford a plumber. Melody asked him if she had come on to him or did he come on to her. She wanted to know if anything had happen while he was over there. Calvin told her that nothing happened. As she was lying down in the bed trying to go to sleep, she was thinking to herself that something did actually happen. The reason why she felt like something happened was because he came home smelling like perfume, and he had lip stick on his shirt. She did not let him know that she saw the lipstick on his shirt. So that is the reason why she was having the feeling that he cheated on her.

So the next day, when Melody was at work, the man that gave her all the encouragement, Brian, walked in. He wanted to know how Melody was doing. She said that everything was fine, but Brian did not believe that. He told her that she was not the same person. There is something that Melody doesn't know about Brian. He is a serious liar. He told her that he had a dream that her husband was over this woman's house. He was supposed to be fixing the plumbing but he ended up doing something else. He told her that her husband and this woman were having sex. He said that her husband did not leave the house until 9:15 pm and arrived home about 9:30 pm.

Immediately, Melody started crying. She believed every word that Brian had said because she knew that no one could have told him this. But the reason that Brian knew that information was because he had been watching her and her husband. Brian wanted Calvin's wife and he was just waiting for the perfect opportunity to get her. When she got home that evening, she confronted Calvin. She had asked him why did he cheat on her? He told her that he went over to Jessica's house to fix the plumbing and afterwards he came home. His wife did not believe him because of what Brian had told her that he saw in his dream. She asked him again why he cheated on her. Calvin could not understand why his wife would assume that he cheated on her. He explained to his wife that nothing happened but she did not believe him.

Given that she was so upset with her husband, she decided to go over to her friend Karen's house. As she pulled up in Karen's drive way, she saw many cars parked on the grass. She knocked on the door and Karen opened the door. Melody asked her what was going on. Karen told her that she was having a get together. Melody told Karen that she really needed to talk with her. So they went into a private room in the house to talk. Melody told her everything that was going on. She asked Karen could she stay the night and Karen told her she could.

After talking with Karen, Melody decided to get herself a glass of punch. As she walked into the kitchen she saw Brian. Brian had asked her how everything was going and she told him that things were not going to well. She told him that she had confronted her husband and he denied everything. Brian asked her if she would like to go somewhere private to talk and she said yes. So they went into Karen's den to talk. Brian knew that Melody was very vulnerable and he took advantage of it. Melody started crying and Brian put his arm around her. He took his hand and grabbed her chin and raised her head up to gaze into her eyes. Brian started kissing on her which led to them having sexual intercourse.

Meanwhile, Calvin called Jessica and told her that his wife was accusing him of sleeping with her. Jessica said that if there is anything she could do to fix the problem, let her know. Calvin began to worry about his wife because it was getting late and his wife did not come home. So he started driving around the city looking for her. Every place that he thought that she could be, he went. After searching for two hours, he finally found her at Karen's house. He knocked on the door and a guest answered. When he went into the house, he asked where his wife was. No one was able to tell him so he went into every room searching for her. Finally, he arrived at the den and opened the door. He couldn't believe that his wife was sleeping with another man. Calvin's stomach dropped. He was so upset that he wanted to kill the both of them. Instead, he turned around and went back home.

Later on that day, Melody came home. She told him the reason that she had cheated on him was because he had cheated on her. Calvin told her that he did not cheat on her; he just fixed Jessica's plumbing. The deacon was extremely hurt because of what his wife had done. Although he was having thoughts about being with other people, he never acted out his thoughts because he knew that it would be wrong. His wife still did not believe that he did not cheat on her. Calvin told her that they really needed to pray about their situation. He told her that they needed to pray that God will show his wife in a dream if he cheated or not. So, they prayed together.

As Melody slept, she had a dream. There were two parts to her dream. In the first part of her dream, God showed her that her husband was at Jessica's house fixing the plumbing. In the second part of her dream, God showed her that Brian lied to her. He showed her in such a way that Brian's goal was to sleep with her. When she woke up that morning tears were flowing down her face. She started crying out to God for forgiveness. After asking God for forgiveness she turned to her husband and asked him to forgive her. Although Calvin was hurt, he forgave his wife.

Every night they prayed to God that he would heal their relationship. Also, they went to the pastor of their church and asked him would he go into prayer with them so that God would mend their broken relationship. After praying consistently for five months, the relationship started to heal. Their relationship ended up being stronger than it was before. Because they took their situation to God in prayer, he mended their relationship back together.

Chapter 7

Using prayer to make decisions

"One of those days Jesus went out to a mountainside to pray, and spent the night praying to God. When morning came, he called his disciples to him and chose twelve of them, whom he also designated apostles"(Luke 6:12-13 NIV).

Before Jesus made an important decision, He took time out for prayer. He went to the mountainside alone to pray to His father. Whenever you have to make decisions in your life, always take time out to talk with the Father in heaven. Go somewhere quiet and pray to your Father so He can lead you in making the best decision you can make.

I remember a young man who would buy everything that he wanted without consulting God about it. Eventually, he ended up filing for bankruptcy because he did not handle his finances wisely. Not once did he pray about things before he purchased them. Always consult God about everything and you will not go wrong. God will not stir you in the wrong direction.

"Then they returned to Jerusalem from the hill called the Mount of Olives, a Sabbath day's walk from the city. When they arrived, they went upstairs to the room where they were staying. Those present were Peter, John, James, and Andrew; Philip and Thomas, Bartholomew and Matthew; James son of Alphaeus and Simon the Zealot, and Judas son of James. They all joined together constantly in

prayer, along with the women and Mary the mother of Jesus, and with his brothers" (Acts 1:12-14 NIV).

The disciples waited and prayed while waiting on the Holy Spirit. Jesus had told them before He was taken up into heaven that they would be baptized with the Holy Spirit. So they all waited and prayed. Whenever you need to make an important decision or face a difficult task, your first priority needs to be prayer. Pray for the Holy Spirit's power and guidance.

Chapter 8

Don't let guilt feelings over sin keep you from praying

"Then Samson prayed to the Lord, 'O Sovereign Lord, remember me. O God, please strengthen me just once more, and let me with one blow get revenge on the Philistines for my two eyes.' Then Samson reached toward the two central pillars on which the temple stood. Bracing himself against them, his right hand on the one and his left hand on the other, Samson said, 'Let me die with the Philistines!' Then he pushed with all his might, and down came the temple on the rulers and all the people in it. Thus he killed many more when he died than while he lived" (Judges 16:28-30 NIV).

In spite of Samson's past, God answered his prayer by destroying the pagan temple and worshipers. God was willing to listen to Samson's prayer of confession and repentance. As a result, God decided to use Samson one more time. One of the effects that sin has is keeping us from feeling like praying. Don't let guilt feelings over sin keep you from going to God for restoration. It doesn't matter how long you have been away from God, God wants to hear from you and restore you to a right relationship with Him. If God could still work in Samson's situation, he can definitely work in yours.